T0145286

The Adventures of Chingy

in New York City!

Charlie Gonzalez

To order additional copies of this book, contact:
Xlibris
844-714-8691
www.Xlibris.com
Orders@Xlibris.com

ISBN: Softcover   978-1-6698-1997-4
           EBook   978-1-6698-1998-1

Print information available on the last page

Rev. date: 12/20/2022

THE ADVENTURES OF CHINGY
IN NEW YORK CITY!

¡LAS AVENTURAS DE CHINGY EN
LA CIUDAD DE NUEVA YORK!

LE AVVENTURE DI CHINGY A
CITTA DI NEW YORK!

Chingy 9/1/13 - 8/10/22

Chingy lived a full life filled
with a lot of love, happiness
and adventure!

CHINGY' BIOGRAPHY:

NAME: CHINGY
HEIGHT: 5 inches
WEIGHT: 31 ounces
AGE: 8 years old
BIRTHDATE: September 1, 2013
BREED: Micro-Chihuahua
FAVORITE FOOD: White meat - chicken & turkey
ORIGIN: Villa Palmeras in San Juan, Puerto Rico

PLACES LIVED:
San Juan, Puerto Rico 2013-2015
Naples, Florida 2015-2017
Bronx, New York 2017-Present

ENGLISH: Chingy arrives in New York City from Naples, Florida!

SPANISH: ¡Chingy llega a la ciudad de Nueva York desde Napoles, Florida!

ITALIAN: Chingy arriva a città di New York City!

ENGLISH: Chingy going to Grandma's house!

SPANISH: ¡Chingy yendo a la casa de la abuela en el Bronx!

ITALIAN: Chingy andando a casa della nonna nel Bronx!

ENGLISH: At home with Grandma and cousin, Shai! (pronounced Shy)

SPANISH: ¡En casa con la abuela y el primo, Shai!

ITALIAN: A casa con la nonna e il cugino, Shai!

At home with Grandma and cousin, Shai! (pronounced Shy)

ENGLISH: Chingy at the doctor's office!

SPANISH: ¡Chingy en el consultorio del médico!

ITALIAN: Chingy presso l'ufficio dei medici!

ENGLISH: "Look at that little dog!"

SPANISH: "¡Mira ese perrito!"

ITALIAN: "Guarda quel cagnolino!

ENGLISH: Chingy at Pelham Park with his Cane Corsi friend!

SPANISH: ¡Chingy en el parque de Pelham Bay con su Cane Corsi amigo!

ITALIAN: Chingy {also} Pelham Bay Park con il suo amico di canna corsi!

ENGLISH: "He's so cute, can I take a picture with him?"

SPANISH: "El es tan lindo, puedo tomarme una foto con el?"

ITALIAN: "Lui é cosi carino, posso fare una foto?"

ENGLISH: Chingy loves going to the beach on a beautiful, sunny day!

SPANISH: ¡A Chingy le encanta ir a la playa en un dia hermosa y soleado!

ITALIAN: Chingy ama andare in spiaggia in una bella giornata di sole!

ENGLISH: "That is the smallest dog I've ever seen!"

SPANISH: "¡Ese es el perro mas pequeño que he visto en mi vida!"

ITALIAN: "Questo é il cane piu piccolo che abbia mai visto!"

ENGLISH: "Oh my God, what a cute little dog!"

SPANISH: "¡Ay dios mío, que lindo perrito!"

ITALIAN: "Dio mio, che simpatico cagnolino!"

ENGLISH: Chingy loves Nathan's hot dogs at Coney Island!

SPANISH: ¡A Chingy le encantan los hot dogs de Nathan's en Coney Island!

ITALIAN: Chingy ama gli hot dog di Nathan's a Coney Island!

Chingy loves
Nathan's hot dogs!

ENGLISH: "What kind of dog is that? Can we take a picture with him?"

SPANISH: "¿Qué clase de perro es ese? Podemos tomarnos un foto con el?"

ITALIAN: "Che razza di cane è? Possiamo fare una foto con lui?"

ENGLISH: Chingy enjoying a beautiful sunny day at Coney Island in Brooklyn, New York!

SPANISH: ¡Chingy disfrutando de un dia soleado en Coney Island en Brooklyn, Nueva York!

ITALIAN: Chingy godendo di una bella giornata di sole a Coney Island a Brooklyn, New York!

ENGLISH: "Oh my God! He's so little! Can I hold him?"

SPANISH: "¡Ay Dios mío! Es tan pequeño! Puedo abrazarlo?"

ITALIAN: "Oh mio Dio! É cosi piccolo! Posso tenerlo?"

ENGLISH: Chingy is a big star at the Puerto Rican Day parade!

SPANISH: ¡Chingy es una gran estrella en el defile del diá de Puerto Rico!

ITALIAN: Chingy è una grande star alla parata del giorno Portoricano!

ENGLISH: Chingy in Flushing, Queens!

SPANISH: Chingy en Flushing, Queens!

ITALIAN: Chingy in Flushing, Queens!

ENGLISH: "He's so cute! Can I have him? What kind of dog is that?"

SPANISH: "¡El es tan lindo! Puedo tenerlo? Que clase de perro es ese?"

ITALIAN: "Lui è così carino, posso averlo? Che razza di Cane è?"

ENGLISH: "That little dog is fearless?"

SPANISH: "¡Ese perrito no tiene miedo!"

ITALIAN: "Quel cagnolino non ha paura!"

ENGLISH: Chingy also goes to church!

SPANISH: Chingy también va a la iglesia!

ITALIAN: Chingy va anche in chiesa!

ENGLISH: Jayla with Chingy!

SPANISH: Jayla con Chingy!

ITALIAN: Jayla con Chingy!

ENGLISH: "That's the most adorable thing I've ever seen!"

SPANISH: "¡Eso es lo más adorable que he visto en mi vida!"

ITALIAN: "Questa é la cosa più adorabile che abbia mai!"

ENGLISH: Chingy walking in midtown Manhattan! Chingy is not afraid of the big city!

SPANISH: ¡Chingy caminando en midtown Manhattan! Chingy no le teme a la gran ciudad!

ITALIAN: Chingy non ha paura della grande citta!

ENGLISH: Chingy also has his mask!

SPANISH: ¡Chingy también tiene su mascara!

ITALIAN: Chingy ha anche la sua marchers!

ENGLISH: Chingy going home on the number 6 train to Pelham Bay in the Bronx!

SPANISH: ¡Chingy regresa a casa en el tren n. 6 a Pelham Bay en el Bronx!

ITALIAN: Chingy tornare a casa sul treno n. 6 per Pelham Bay nel Bronx!

ENGLISH: Chingy at home in his bed after a long, busy and exciting day in the big city!

SPANISH: ¡Chingy en casa en su Cama despues de un largo, ajetreado y emocionante dia en la gran ciudad!

ITALIAN: Chingy a casa a nel suo letto dopo una giornata lunga, impegnativa ed emozionate nella grande citta!

ENGLISH: New York City loves Chingy and Chingy loves New York City!

SPANISH: ¡La ciudad de Nueva York ama a Chingy y Chingy ama a la ciudad de Nueva York!

ITALIAN: New York City ama Chingy e Chingy ama New York City!

New York City loves Chingy and Chingy loves New York City!

Charlie Gonzalez

Chicago